Mary Kingsley

Struan Reid

www.heinemann.co.uk/library
Visit our website to find out more information about **Heinemann Library** books.

To order:
 Phone 44 (0) 1865 888066
 Send a fax to 44 (0) 1865 314091
💻 Visit the Heinemann Bookshop at www.heinemann.co.uk/library to browse our
catalogue and order online.

First published in Great Britain by Heinemann Library,
Halley Court, Jordan Hill, Oxford OX2 8EJ,
a division of Reed Educational and Professional Publishing Ltd.
Heinemann is a registered trademark of Reed Educational and Professional Publishing Ltd.

OXFORD MELBOURNE AUCKLAND
JOHANNESBURG BLANTYRE GABORONE
IBADAN PORTSMOUTH (NH) USA CHICAGO

Designed by AMR
Illustrated by Art Construction
Originated by Ambassador Litho Ltd
Printed by Wing King Tong

ISBN 0 431 10491 3
06 05 04 03 02
10 9 8 7 6 5 4 3 2 1

British Library Cataloguing in Publication Data
Reid, Struan
Mary Kingsley. – (Groundbreakers)
1.Kingsley, Mary H. (Mary Henrietta), 1862–1900 2.Women
explorers – Great Britain – Biography – Juvenile literature
3.Explorers – Great Britain – Biography – Juvenile literature
I.Title
916'.6'04'092

Acknowledgements
The publishers would like to thank the following for permission to reproduce photographs:
British Museum: pp. 26, 40; Caroline Penn/Impact: p. 17; Collections: p. 9; Collections/John
Miller: p. 14; Corbis/Francoise D. Mulder: p. 18; Courtesy of Beatrice de Cardi: p. 8; Dundee
City Council, Central Library, Photographic Collection: p. 23; Highgate Literary and Scientific
Institution: pp. 6, 7, 41; Hulton: pp. 11, 15, 31, 33, 35, 37; Mary Evans: pp. 4, 5, 10; Master and
Fellows of Trinity College Cambridge: p. 32; National Maritime Museum: p. 16; Pitt-Rivers
Museum, Oxford: pp. 20, 21; Robert Harding: pp. 12, 13, 19, 24, 29; Royal Commonwealth
Society; p. 22; Royal Geographical Society: p. 34; Simonstown Museum: pp. 36, 38, 39; Sue
Cunningham: pp. 25, 27; Topham: pp. 28, 30.

Cover photograph reproduced with permission of Mary Evans.

Every effort has been made to contact copyright holders of any material reproduced in this
book. Any omissions will be rectified in subsequent printings if notice is given to the publishers.

Our thanks to Christopher Gibb for his comments in the preparation of this book.

Any words appearing in the text in bold, **like this**, are explained in the glossary.

Contents

An adventurer in Africa   4

A lonely childhood   6

Teaching herself   8

The dutiful daughter   10

A taste of Africa   12

A new life   14

Sailing away   16

Journey inland   18

Return to the coast   20

The second expedition   22

To the mouth of the Ogowé   24

Among the Fang   26

The Throne of Thunder   28

Return to England   30

A political figure   32

To Africa again   34

A nurse once more   36

Death in South Africa   38

The legacy of Mary Kingsley   40

Map of Mary Kingsley's journeys   42

Timeline   44

Places to visit and further reading 45

Glossary   46

Index   48

An adventurer in Africa

You can follow the routes of Mary Kingsley's journeys on the map on pages 42–3.

Mary Kingsley was an English explorer who became the first European to visit parts of Gabon in West Africa. Her father, a doctor, spent most of his married life abroad and her mother had to bring up Mary and her younger brother Charles on her own. Mary had a very lonely and isolated childhood and there were few visitors to the family home.

When Mary's parents died in 1892, she found that she was suddenly free to enjoy her own interests, after a lifetime of duty to her parents. The following year she set out on the first of two journeys to West Africa. When she returned from her second expedition, she published a book called *Travels in West Africa*. This was a bestseller and almost overnight Mary Kingsley became one of the most famous people in the country, much in demand as a public speaker.

At this time, during the 1890s, the powerful countries of Europe were in the middle of their 'scramble for Africa' and huge territories were claimed as **colonies** by Britain, France, Belgium, Italy and Germany.

More than any other well-known person of the time, Mary Kingsley influenced public opinion about Africa by presenting a positive yet balanced picture of the continent and its people.

A photograph of Mary Kingsley in 1897. She had returned to England from her travels in West Africa two years earlier and had become one of the most famous people in the country.

Mary loved adventure and travel, but after her second expedition she decided she should stay in England and fight for the rights of the African people. She was not afraid to stand up to powerful politicians, and from 1895 until 1900 she tried to convince the British government to make fundamental changes to the way they ruled the new African colonies.

In Mary Kingsley's words:

'Whatever we do in Africa today, a thousand years hence there will be Africans to thrive or suffer for it.'

(Written in a pamphlet entitled *The Story of West Africa*)

Even if she had not become the champion of the African people, Mary Kingsley would still be regarded as one of the great names of **Victorian** England. The two books she wrote describing her journeys are among the best travel books ever written in the English language. Her bravery, combined with her sympathy for and understanding of African people and their way of life, made her one of the greatest of all the European travellers in that region.

Mary Kingsley (to the left of the flag) travelling in a dugout canoe on the Ogowé River.

Mary Henrietta Kingsley was born in Islington, North London on 13 October 1862. She was the eldest child of Dr George Kingsley and Mary Bailey Kingsley. Her father was a medical doctor who was happier accompanying expeditions to remote parts of the world than setting up a **practice** in England. He was away travelling for most of Mary's childhood and, as a result, his daughter regarded him more as an exotic and fascinating visitor than the head of the family.

Dr George Kingsley, Mary's father. This photograph was taken shortly before his marriage to Mary Bailey in 1862.

Shutting out the world

The Kingsleys were a well-known, **middle-class** family in **Victorian** England. Mary's grandfather had been a **clergyman**, as was her uncle Charles Kingsley, who was also a famous **social reformer**, **novelist** and poet. Mary's mother, however, came from a **working-class** family called Bailey and she was the daughter of an innkeeper. She had once been the Kingsley family's cook.

UNCLE HENRY

One of the few visitors to the family home was Mary's uncle, Henry Kingsley (1830–76). As a young man he had worked as a gold **prospector** in Australia. Mary loved to listen to his stories about this different and exciting world, and when Henry died of cancer aged only 46 she lost a trusted friend and adviser.

The class differences between the Kingsley and Bailey families would not matter to us today, but in the 19th century right up to the early part of the 20th century, people's social backgrounds mattered a great deal. Men and women from different social classes rarely married each other.

The family moved from Islington to nearby Highgate when Mary was one year old. In 1866, Mrs Kingsley gave birth to another child, a boy named Charles (Charley). With her husband constantly away, she led a very isolated life with her young children. Sometimes she would help a sick neighbour, but otherwise she shut the door of her house firmly against the world. Instead of receiving visitors and friends, Mrs Kingsley kept a **menagerie** of animals – cats, dogs and a cockerel – as companions in the house. Mary was expected to help her mother with the household **chores** from her earliest years. At the age of ten, she was in charge of keeping the house clean.

Number 22 Southwood Lane in Highgate. This was the house the Kingsley family moved to in 1864 and they were to live there for fifteen years.

Teaching herself

Mary grew up believing her duty in life was to serve others, but once her household **chores** were finished for the day, she retreated into a world of books. Dr Kingsley's library provided his bright young daughter with a rich source of interest and learning.

Growing interests

Mary was never sent to school and was completely self-educated. From a very young age she became passionately interested in science. This would have been remarkable for any girl in **Victorian** times, when many families considered it unnecessary for women to be educated at all, let alone in science. She taught herself mathematics and learned all sorts of useful skills like carpentry and plumbing. It took a great effort to educate herself, but she was rarely discouraged. However, she must have been hurt that her father spent large sums of money on the education of her brother Charley but nothing on herself.

A miniature portrait of Mary Kingsley as a young girl. It gives an idea of her pale, fragile appearance when she was growing up.

In 1879, the Kingsleys moved from London to Bexley Heath in Kent. Mrs Kingsley was not well and it was thought moving out of the city would do her good. Young Charley was sent to a local school but Mary stayed at home and helped her mother. Seven years later the family moved again, to Cambridge.

In the words of a family friend:

'A thin, pale girl of middle height, with straight fair hair and blue eyes, quiet and domestic habits.'

(A description of Mary when she was 17, by one of her father's friends)

Charley, aged 20, had been accepted to study law at Christ's College at the university there.

Mary was then 24 years old. Their father had retired and lived permanently in England. As a result, there was now a constant stream of visitors to the family house in Mortimer Road, Cambridge. Many visitors were impressed by Mary's confidence and intelligence: 'She belonged to the order of native-born genius, which cannot be classified,' wrote one. She met many interesting people and became friends with several brilliant historians, **archaeologists** and **physicians**.

Until the end of the 19th century, women could not attend university, but at the time when Mary and her family went to live in Cambridge, in the 1880s, a number of exciting developments were taking place in the world of women's education. Two of the university colleges, called Newnham and Girton, were beginning to run courses for women and some years later women began to be accepted as full-time university students.

A view of Cambridge today. When the Kingsley family moved there in 1886 Mary met many well-known scholars who worked at the University.

The dutiful daughter

In 1888, Mary Kingsley was 26 years old, and for the first time her life seemed to be expanding beyond the narrow confines of her family demands. That year she even travelled abroad for the first time when she visited Paris for a week with a family friend.

Looking after the family

Just as Mary was beginning to spread her wings, she had to return to family responsibilities. These took over her life so completely she never considered getting married, which would have been usual for a woman of her age at that time. Soon after Mary returned from Paris her mother had a **stroke** which left her paralysed. For the next four years, Mary nursed her mother through the day and often through the night. Although she had never trained as a nurse, she carried out the work with her usual devotion.

A painting of the Rue de la Paix in Paris in about 1890. When Mary visited the city, she had her first taste of freedom from family responsibilities.

Mary's father and brother gave her no help. They took it for granted she would continue to run the household and look after everyone. Soon after, Dr Kingsley also became ill with **rheumatic fever**, which weakened his heart. To aid his recovery he went on a voyage round the world, but on his return some months later his heart was so weak that he too needed nursing.

On the morning of 2 February 1892, Mary went up to her father's bedroom with his post as usual and found him dead in bed. He was 65 years old and had died from a heart attack. Ten weeks after her father was buried, Mary's mother also died in her sleep. From now on Mary would always wear black clothes in mourning for her parents.

In Mary Kingsley's words:

'It was years of work and watching and anxiety, a narrower life in home interests than ever, and a more hopelessly depressing one, for it was a losing fight with death the whole time.'

(Taken from *In the Days of my Youth*)

A SHOCKING DISCOVERY

As Mary was sorting through her parents' papers, she came across their marriage certificate. The date of the marriage was given as 9 October 1862. This was just a few days before her birth. This sudden discovery of her parents' 'shotgun wedding' and that she had nearly been **illegitimate** must have been a great shock to Mary. It also helped explain her father's long absences abroad and the fact that few Kingsley relations ever bothered to visit her mother.

This photograph of Mary Kingsley was taken for a newspaper article about her in 1895. It shows her dressed in her characteristic black clothes.

A taste of Africa

Mary Kingsley was nearly 30 years old when her parents died. Her father had left some money that was now inherited by his two children. This gave Mary a good income of £500 a year, roughly equivalent to £30,000 today. She would now have enough money to live off without having to work and some to spare for luxuries.

Island exploration

The first thing she wanted to do as soon as she could was get away and rest. She was not interested in visiting holiday resorts in Britain or continental Europe but had set her heart instead on Africa, one of the places her father had travelled to. Mary had read her father's detailed notes of what he saw there and was eager to go there herself. For her first trip, however, she decided to travel to the Canary Islands off the north-west coast of Africa. She looked on this as a preparation for her eventual travels in Africa.

YOU CAN LOCATE THE PLACES MARY KINGSLEY VISITED ON THE MAP ON PAGES 42–3.

The journey by ship from England to the Canaries took a week. Stopping first at Tenerife, the ship sailed on to Lanzarote and then to Grand Canary. Kingsley stayed much longer on the islands than she had originally planned. She travelled from one

Approaching the island of Tenerife, Kingsley was impressed by its magnificent volcanic peak rising up in the blazing sunshine.

island to another, often paddling across in canoes. One of her most exciting trips took her to the little-known volcanic island of Gomera.

The Canaries were an important port of call for most ships travelling from Europe to West Africa. Kingsley made a number of expeditions to the coast of Africa on some of these ships. During her crossings over and back again, she heard many stories from her fellow passengers about the sights, and dangers, of Africa. By the time she finally returned to England in autumn 1892, she had made up her mind to travel to West Africa as soon as possible.

One of the people Kingsley befriended on her journeys from the Canaries to West Africa was James Batty (1868–1946). He was a businessman and gold trader in West Africa and eventually married Kingsley's great friend Violet Roy. His descriptions of West Africa enticed Kingsley to travel there herself.

In Mary Kingsley's words:

'[The boats travelled] … on their way out with iron bedsteads, … candles, and salt petre, on their way home with black people of all ages and sexes, monkeys, parrots, snakes, canary birds, sheep, palm oil, gold dust and ivory.'

(Kingsley's description of the boats travelling between the Canary Islands and West Africa, from a letter to her friend Hatty Johnson)

A view of the small volcanic island of Gomera in the Canaries. Kingsley missed the boat back to Grand Canary and had to spend the night sleeping rough on the island.

A new life

Mary Kingsley returned from her holiday in the Canaries to a cold, damp English autumn. As she sat in the small flat in West London she had moved into with her brother Charley, she began to make plans to leave for Africa. She contacted the British Museum of Natural History, and the Keeper of **Zoology**, Dr Albert Günther, paid her a small sum to make a collection of fish and insects during her travels. She bought a revolver (a pistol, which she never had to use), and wrote letters to anyone she thought might be able to provide her with useful contacts in Africa.

Looking after Charley

It was to be another year, however, before Mary could finally leave. Charley seemed incapable of making up his mind what he wanted to do. He had finished his studies at Cambridge University and now had an idea to travel to the **Far East** to study Chinese **philosophy**. While he was in England, however, Mary felt obliged to look after him. 'I came home to look after him domestically as long as he wants me to do so. I must do it – it is duty – the religion I was brought up in,' Kingsley wrote to a friend.

The main entrance to the Natural History Museum in London. The museum opened in 1881. Twelve years later, Mary Kingsley contacted Dr Günther in the Zoology Department.

In Mary Kingsley's words:

'And then, when the fight was lost, when there were no more odd jobs anyone wanted me to do at home, I, out of my life in books ... had to go to West Africa ... doing odd jobs and trying to understand things, pursuing knowledge under difficulties with unbroken devotion.'

(From Kingsley's famous book *Travels in West Africa*)

As Charley dithered, Mary continued to find out all she could about West Africa.

Finally, in June 1893, Charley left for the Far East and Mary set off at last. She travelled to the port of Liverpool loaded with luggage and heavy glass jars and medical spirit for preserving fish. On 2 August 1893, Mary Kingsley, the quiet and dutiful daughter and sister, set sail on the SS (steam ship) *Lagos* for what was considered one of the most dangerous places in the world.

The Customs House and docks at Liverpool in the late 19th century. When Mary Kingsley sailed from here in 1893, the port was one of the largest and most important in the world.

CHARLES KINGSLEY

Mary's brother Charley (1866–1909) was always a disappointment to her. He was just as selfish and demanding as their father, but had none of their father's adventurous spirit that Mary so admired. Charley was also very lazy – although he had ambitions to become a writer, he never completed work on his father's papers. He also had promised a biography of Mary, but never even started writing it!

Sailing away

Within days of leaving England, Mary Kingsley had made friends with Captain Murray, who was in charge of the *Lagos*. He had been sailing ships to 'the Coast', as West Africa was known, for 30 years. He told Kingsley all about the places she planned to visit. Fellow passengers told more colourful tales about deadly snakes and crocodiles, terrifying diseases and **cannibals**.

SS Lagos *at about the time Kingsley sailed in her. The* Lagos *was a small cargo ship rather than a passenger liner and it was cramped and not very comfortable inside.*

'THE WHITE MAN'S GRAVE'

West Africa at this time had a terrible reputation for death and disease. It was known as 'the white man's grave' because so many Europeans died there. Here is part of a conversation Kingsley overheard on board the *Lagos*: "Do you get anything else but fever down there?" asks a newcomer nervously. "Haven't time as a general rule, but I have known some fellows get kraw kraw … Portuguese itch, abcesses, ulcers, the Guinea worm and the smallpox [various diseases found in Africa at the time]," observe the chorus calmly.'

Down the coast

From the Canaries the ship sailed south past the Cape Verde Islands on the western coast of Africa. Kingsley enjoyed the beautiful clear weather and the sight of dolphins swimming beside the ship. As the coast of Africa came into distant view, however, the weather changed dramatically. August was the worst month to travel to 'the Coast' as it is the rainy season. The *Lagos* was hit by a **tornado**.

On 17 August, Captain Murray dropped anchor off the coast of Sierra Leone. They could go no further because of the thick fog that hung around the *Lagos* like a wet blanket. The next morning, the fog lifted and Kingsley saw the breathtaking beauty of the coastline and the lovely port of Freetown. All the sights of Africa she had spent years reading about now began to unfold before her eyes.

In Mary Kingsley's words:

'I knew the place so well. Yes; there were all the bays, Kru, English and Pirate; and the mountains, whose thunder rumbling caused Pedro do Centra to call the place Sierra Leone [Lion Mountains] when he discovered it in 1462.'

(Kingsley's description of her first sight of Freetown. Pedro do Centra was a Portuguese explorer, and later European explorers named the bays.)

YOU CAN FOLLOW MARY KINGSLEY'S JOURNEYS ON THE MAP ON PAGES 42–3.

After a short stay in Freetown, the *Lagos* continued its journey, passing the Bights (bays) of Benin, Biafra and the Gold Coast. Whenever the ship dropped anchor in a port, Kingsley would get off and visit the coast nearby. In early September, the *Lagos* reached Sao Paulo de Loanda (Luanda), now part of Angola.

A view of Freetown, Sierra Leone, today. Kingsley first arrived there on market day and she loved walking round the colourful stalls that sold fruit and vegetables grown inland.

Journey inland

As they sailed down the coast of Africa, Kingsley caught tantalizing glimpses of the landscape inland. She was determined to travel through the countryside herself and to study the religion and customs of the people who lived there. She left the *Lagos* in Luanda and said goodbye to Captain Murray and her other shipmates.

A photograph of the modern city of Luanda. Founded by the Portuguese in 1575, it is now the capital city of Angola.

Paddling and walking

After some weeks in Luanda and the surrounding area, Kingsley travelled north to the town of Cabinda in the French Congo (now known as Gabon). While there she met a remarkable Englishman called Richard Dennett, who told her all about the religions and customs of the people further inland. From Cabinda, she travelled into the neighbouring Congo Free State (now the Democratic Republic of Congo), where the **indigenous** people were under the brutal control of King Leopold of the Belgians. At the mouth of the mighty Congo River, she rejoined the *Lagos* and travelled upstream to Matadi.

RICHARD DENNETT

Richard Dennett (1857–1921) was the son of an English vicar. When Kingsley met him in Cabinda he had been working for 18 years as a trader for the English company of Hatton and Cookson. He had married a local woman and had made extensive studies of the people he lived amongst. Five years after they met, Kingsley wrote the introduction to a book Dennett wrote on the local people, called *Folklore of the Fjort*.

From Matadi, Kingsley travelled for about two months on foot or by canoe, often through thick forest and swamp, and mostly alone, back into the French Congo. Reaching Libreville, capital city of the French Congo, she went to the nearby port of Glass, where she boarded the SS *La Rochelle* bound for England. The ship made stops in Cameroon and then the port of Calabar (in what is now Nigeria), where she met the Governor, Sir Claude MacDonald. The closer she got to home after her five-month trip, the more she longed to return to the wonderful sights and sounds of the Africa she had left behind.

In Mary Kingsley's words:

'The method of progression was ... varied – hammocks, canoes and walking .... A whole world grows up gradually out of the gloom before your eyes. Snakes, beetles, bats and beasts people the region ....'

(Kingsley's description of her trek through the forests of the French Congo, from a letter to her friend Violet Roy)

YOU CAN FOLLOW MARY KINGSLEY'S JOURNEYS ON THE MAP ON PAGES 42–3.

Libreville, which Kingsley visited in 1893, was built on a range of hills overlooking a well-sheltered port. It is now the capital city of Gabon. The city takes its name (meaning 'free town') from a settlement founded by freed slaves in 1849.

Return to the coast

The *La Rochelle* docked in Liverpool on a cold, grey evening in January 1894 and Kingsley travelled south by train to London. She returned to her top-floor flat and immediately started wondering what on earth she was doing back in London. The cloudy, dull sky contrasted so much with the warmth and brilliant colours she had left behind in Africa.

Keeping memories alive

She tried in a number of different ways to keep her recent experiences in Africa alive. She decorated the small flat with objects and souvenirs she had brought back with her – brightly woven cloths, painted masks and bronze bangles.

Mary Kingsley's experience of the world had changed through her independent travels. However, her brother Charley, who had recently returned from his own travels in the **Far East**, still expected his sister to look after him. Mary was to remain in England for most of 1894 as Charley's housekeeper.

Kingsley brought back this sculpture, which she named Muvungu, from her first visit to Africa.

EARLY WRITINGS

Another way in which Kingsley kept her African memories fresh and alive was to write about her experiences. She had made masses of notes on her first journey and she used these to start writing a book that she called *The Bights of Benin*. This was never published, but it was later to form the basis of her best-selling work *Travels in West Africa*.

Soon, however, events conspired to take Kingsley back to her beloved Africa. Dr Günther at the British Museum was so impressed upon seeing her first collection of African fish and other specimens that he immediately **commissioned** her to collect freshwater fish from the region between the Niger and Congo rivers. Kingsley also received a message from Lady MacDonald, wife of Sir Claude, whom she had met in Calabar. Lady MacDonald was planning to join her husband in Africa and invited Kingsley to travel over with her. Mary leapt at this invitation, particularly as Charley had recently left for Singapore. On Sunday, 23 December 1894, the SS *Batanga* steamed out of Liverpool with Kingsley on board. Her spirits soared, as she felt she was returning to her true home.

In Mary Kingsley's words:

'The charm of Africa is a painful one. It gives you pleasure to fall under it when you are out there, but when you are back here it gives you pain by calling you.'

(From a lecture given by Kingsley)

Some of the bronze and brass armlets Kingsley brought from Africa. She used them to decorate the walls of her London flat in 1894.

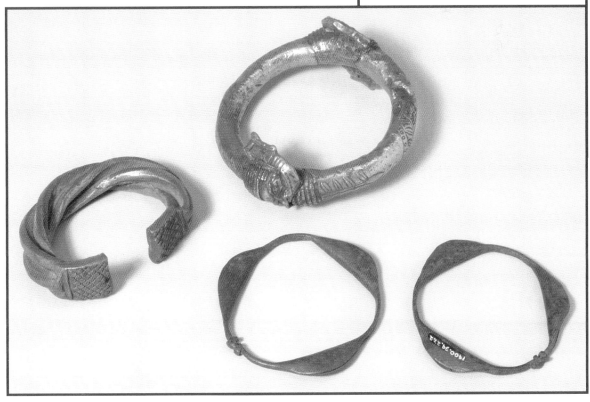

The second expedition

The journey from Liverpool to the first port of call in West Africa took two weeks. Lady MacDonald was at first a little daunted by her scientific travelling companion and felt she should be constantly pointing out 'all sorts of marine objects overboard' to Kingsley. However, the two women got on very well and were soon discussing subjects other than fish! As so many Europeans died from fever and disease at that time, Kingsley admired Lady MacDonald, whose 'courage in going to the Coast was far greater than my own, for she had more to lose had fever claimed her'.

YOU CAN LOCATE CALABAR ON THE MAP ON PAGE 43.

A colonial life

Towards the end of February 1895, the *Batanga* at last reached Calabar, where the women were greeted by a wonderful fireworks display organized by Sir Claude MacDonald. Soon after their arrival, Sir Claude had to leave on a trip to a neighbouring island called Fernando Po. His wife and Kingsley went along with him. The day after they arrived, Kingsley set out alone to explore the island with its grand mountains covered by thick forests. During her short stay there she spent most of the time studying the customs of the **indigenous** Bubis people.

Mary Kingsley (centre) in Calabar in 1895. Lady MacDonald is seated on her right while Sir Claude MacDonald is on her left. Standing behind them are members of Sir Claude's staff.

Back in Calabar, Sir Claude was called away again on another duty. Kingsley stayed behind to keep Lady MacDonald company, assisting her in the official duties of the governor's wife. Kingsley was really more interested in studying the customs of the indigenous people, but this period in Calabar gave her valuable insight into the lives of European women in Africa.

In Mary Kingsley's words:

'I must say the African leopard is an audacious animal, although … I really think … he is the most lovely animal I have ever seen ….'

(Written after defending herself with a chair on being attacked by a leopard on the terrace of a house in Calabar)

MARY SLESSOR

While she was staying with the MacDonalds, Kingsley travelled up the Calabar River to visit a **missionary** called Mary Slessor (1848–1915). This remarkable woman was born in Dundee in Scotland and from the age of eleven worked as a weaver in a mill. As a teenager she began to educate herself by attending night school. Aged 27 she went to Calabar as a missionary and teacher, never having left Scotland before. She quickly learned the local languages and started working with the local women. She adopted many twin children (considered unlucky in that part of Africa) and was highly respected by both the Africans and the Europeans.

A photograph of Mary Slessor, taken in about 1891 when she was 43 years old.

To the mouth of the Ogowé

You can locate the places mentioned on the map on pages 42–3.

By May 1895, the heavy rains had made 'puddling about' in canoes looking for fish very difficult and uncomfortable. It was time to move on. Kingsley said goodbye to the MacDonalds, who had been so kind to her for the past months, and once more boarded the *Batanga*, heading for the French Congo.

Changing ships

In order to reach the French Congo, Kingsley first went northwards to the port of Lagos and then transferred, after a wait, to a second boat, the *Benguella*, which was travelling south.

The main purpose of her trip was to travel up the Ogowé River, the greatest river in Africa between the Niger River and the Congo River. Here, she hoped to find different species of fish in waters away from tidal influence. This was also the wildest and most dangerous part of West Africa. It was covered in thick rainforest and populated by people who lived beyond the control of Europeans and who had a reputation for being fierce warriors.

The port of Lagos, capital city of Nigeria. Kingsley started her journey into Africa from this city, which is now an important industrial centre.

A LOSS OF NERVE

In Lagos, Kingsley had to use a small boat to transport her from the *Batanga* to the *Benguella*. When she caught sight of how filthy the boat was, she was horrified and very nearly decided to sail back to England. 'Rats ran freely everywhere,' she wrote, and most of the African passengers already on board were soaking wet and very ill. She was lowered in a chair down the side of the *Batanga* as the smaller boat bobbed up and down in the rough waters.

Eventually, on 20 May 1895, the *Benguella* sailed into the port of Glass, near Libreville. One morning, two weeks later, Kingsley left her cabin on the *Benguella*, boarded a **paddle steamer** and set out for the Ogowé River. This was to be the start of the most exciting and interesting time of her life. The steamer kept within sight of the coast until late afternoon, when they reached the mouth of the Ogowé. This river travels for more than 1127 kilometres (700 miles) from the heart of Gabon to the Atlantic Ocean and Kingsley described it as looking like 'a broad road of burnished bronze'.

In Mary Kingsley's words:

'The day closed with a dramatic beauty. Dead ahead of us … rose the moon, a great orb of crimson … Right astern, the sun sank down into the mist, … and when he had gone out of view, sent up flushes of amethyst, gold, carmine, and serpent green …'

(Kingsley's description of her arrival at the Ogowé River)

Among the Fang

You can follow the route of Mary Kingsley's journey on the map on pages 42–3.

The boat steamed on up the Ogowé for two days until it reached the island town of Lambaréné. Kingsley stayed two weeks with a French **missionary**, Monsieur Jacot, and his wife. While she was there, Kingsley started to learn the languages of the **indigenous** Fang people she might soon be meeting.

Off again

She left on 22 June on a steamer called the *Eclaireur* and travelled further up the Ogowé: 'We go on up stream; now and again stopping at little villages to land passengers or at little sub-factories to discharge cargo …' After hiring a dugout canoe with a crew of eight Africans to paddle upstream beyond the Ogowé's **rapids**, she returned to Lambaréné to plan her most ambitious expedition yet: a gruelling overland trek through unknown territory between the Ogowé and Remboué rivers, down the Remboué and back to Glass and Libreville. On 22 July 1895, Madame Jacot waved goodbye to Kingsley and her crew of four local men on a route no European had attempted before.

By the first evening, they had reached the small town of Arevooma, and Kingsley spent the night in the home of one of her crew. Early next morning, they paddled westwards along the Orembo-Wango River into the heart of Fang country. The Fang had a fearsome reputation as **cannibals**, but Kingsley found them to be friendly. In their villages, she traded medical supplies and gave nursing help to those affected by disease in return for somewhere to stay and to take notes.

This photograph of Fang men and boys was used to illustrate Kingsley's book Travels in West Africa. *She probably took the photograph herself.*

Some days later, they left their canoe and began to trek overland, through thick mud and over fallen trees in the tropical rainforest. After many adventures, including being covered in blood-sucking leeches, Kingsley at last reached the banks of the Remboué, her final destination.

AN OBJECT OF CURIOSITY

As she walked between villages, Kingsley was an object of great curiosity to the Fang people. Europeans on the African coast thought it extraordinary that a woman should want to travel in this inland area, and the Fang themselves were very surprised to see her. They regarded her as a 'devil-man', as she was always dressed from neck to feet in a thick black dress and wore a neat black bonnet on her head. She carried an umbrella wherever she went and when entering a village would call out: 'It's only me!'

In Mary Kingsley's words:

'This particular village I had arrived at had, guarding its gate, two warriors, splendid creatures, good six-footers, painted, armed with four spears apiece, and having their hair magnificently plaited into horns ....'

(Kingsley's description of her arrival at one of the Fang villages)

A tributary of the Ogowé River. Thick jungle comes right down to the water's edge. Kingsley trekked through similar jungle on her way to the Remboué River.

The Throne of Thunder

You can follow Mary Kingsley's journeys on the map on pages 42–3.

On the Remboué, Kingsley met a local trader called Obanjo, who 'liked [his name] pronounced Captain Johnson'. Her journey back to Glass with this colourful character was to be every bit as exciting as her journey out from Glass. They set out in a rickety old boat that was a cross between a canoe and a sailing boat and Kingsley had a hair-raising trip. At one stage, two Fang boys persuaded 'Captain Johnson' to take them to Libreville. As they sped down the river they were chased by the boys' angry mothers in one canoe and a group of Fang warriors in another.

Time for a few more trips

Exhausted but exhilarated, Kingsley finally arrived back in Glass, with 'all the comforts … and safety associated with it'. She soon set out on another expedition, though, this time to an island called Corisco, about 32 kilometres (20 miles) off the coast of Gabon. She spent two days exploring the island and joined a fishing party of local Coriscan women. Returning to Glass on 8 August 1895, Kingsley's boat was nearly overturned by a passing whale.

A trading station on the Niger River at the time that Mary Kingsley was in West Africa. She made many friends and contacts at places like this.

Mary Kingsley sailed from Glass to Victoria in Cameroon where the magnificent shape of Mungo Mah Lobeh, or 'Throne of Thunder' (now known as Mount Cameroon), loomed over the town. She had decided she would climb the 4200-metre peak and set out with guides on the morning of 20 September. It started to rain as they entered the **foothills**, and the thick forests combined with heavy mists made the climb very difficult. As always, Kingsley was wearing her long dress, and as she climbed higher and higher the sun began to break through the mist and burn her face until it was covered in bleeding blisters.

The climb was an incredible achievement, because above 3000 metres she would have found it very difficult to breathe and it would have been extremely cold. It took them ten days to reach the summit but only two days to stumble down again into Victoria on 28 September.

Mount Cameroon rising majestically from the surrounding land. Kingsley thought the mountain was one of the most beautiful sights she had ever seen and she wanted to 'bow down and worship'.

In Mary Kingsley's words:

'… *the weather has robbed me of my main object in coming here, namely to get a good view and an idea of the way the unexplored mountain range behind Calabar tends.*'

(Kingsley's description of her climb up the Throne of Thunder, the first by a European woman. Views from the summit were spoilt by the mists.)

Return to England

After Kingsley arrived back in Victoria from the Throne of Thunder, she sailed to Calabar. She took time to visit her new friend Mary Slessor. The two women talked excitedly late into the night as Kingsley described her recent adventures among the Fang. These were to be some of the last days she would ever spend in West Africa.

A household name

In the middle of November 1895, Kingsley boarded the *Barkana* at Calabar and set sail for home. The ship sailed north past the coasts of Liberia and Sierra Leone and on to the Canary Islands. Kingsley had been away from England this time for nearly a year and had lived a life of excitement and adventure.

Her life was never to be the same again. News of her incredible journeys in West Africa had already reached England before her and several articles had appeared in newspapers about her adventures. So when the *Barkana* docked in Liverpool on 30 November, Kingsley stepped off the ship as a celebrity.

A view of Kensington High Street, in London in about 1899. Kingsley lived in West Kensington from 1895.

Kingsley was pleased her exploits were reported with such enthusiasm, but she was annoyed that she was also being written about as some sort of freak.

Some people thought she was a strange woman who walked around Africa on her own amongst bloodthirsty savages. People recognized her great achievement but, at the same time, they regarded her with suspicion because women in those days were not expected to do that sort of thing.

Kingsley returned to her flat in West London. Amongst her luggage was her collection of dead fish and insects preserved in jars for the Natural History Museum and an enormous live lizard which she now presented to the Regent's Park Zoo in London. The name of Mary Kingsley was famous throughout the country and everyone seemed to want her company.

AMONG THE GREATEST

Mary Kingsley was now recognized as one of the greatest names in African exploration. Other famous explorers of Africa included James Bruce (1730–94), who travelled from Egypt to Ethiopia; Mungo Park (1771–1806), who went up the River Niger; René Caillié (1799–1838), who travelled to Timbuktu; David Livingstone (1813–73), a Christian **missionary** who trekked right across Africa; and Henry Stanley (1841–1904), who travelled from the east to the west coasts of Africa.

The Scottish missionary David Livingstone, whose name was one of the most famous in African exploration when Mary Kingsley began her travels in West Africa. When he died, his heart was buried in Africa while his body was brought back to England.

For the next five years, Kingsley travelled around Britain giving lectures at schools, colleges and **learned societies**. Large audiences came to her lectures, and she could charge quite high fees, but she often charged nothing in order to support good causes.

A fairer picture

Throughout 1896, Kingsley was busy writing a book about her travels. On 21 January 1897, her *Travels in West Africa* was published and immediately became a bestseller. In the first twelve months after publication, it made over £3000 for the publisher (equivalent to about £180,000 in today's money). It also made a lot of money for Kingsley, and its success led to even more invitations for her to give lectures.

These cartoons of Mary Kingsley were drawn by students at a lecture she gave in Cambridge in 1899. The one on the left was called 'Anticipation' and the one on the right was called 'Realization'.

In Mary Kingsley's words:

'West Africa today is just a quarry of paving-stones for Hell, and those stones are cemented in places with men's blood mixed with wasted gold.'

(From a letter written in 1899 criticizing British rule in West Africa. She felt African lives were being needlessly wasted because the British government did not understand Africa.)

At this time, Britain and many other European countries were carving out vast **empires** across Africa. They wanted African territory because they could make money from the raw materials like rubber, wood and gold that they found there. They sometimes mistreated the African people who worked for them. Kingsley felt strongly that if the British government was ruling parts of Africa, then it must do so only with complete fairness, respecting the customs, religions and ancient traditions of the African people. She wrote letters to newspapers and politicians and hers was one of the few voices to defend the rights of the Africans against British rule.

Kingsley received many invitations to return to Africa. With her great sense of duty, however, she stayed in England, hoping to help change British government policies towards Africa. At this time she also fell ill with a chest infection, but managed to continue her lectures and write a second book. *West African Studies*, published on 31 January 1899, was another great success, described by one reviewer as 'the most valuable contribution on the internal politics of western Africa'.

Joseph Chamberlain, who was appointed Secretary of State for the Colonies in 1895, the year Kingsley returned from Africa.

JOSEPH CHAMBERLAIN

The most powerful of all the politicians Kingsley wrote to at this time was the British Secretary of State for the **Colonies**, Joseph Chamberlain (1836–1914). He devoted his life to social reform at home in Britain and to the strengthening of the British Empire abroad. Kingsley's letters to him helped make the British government more aware of the customs and traditions of African people.

Throughout 1899 Kingsley became increasingly frustrated – the longer she stayed in England, the more she craved Africa. However, she continued with her hectic schedule of lectures promoting her experiences of Africa. Her brother was also living with her again and making further demands on her time and energy.

Africa calling

During 1899, the second Boer War broke out in South Africa. With her experience of nursing her own family and also sick people in West African villages, Kingsley applied to the British **War Office** to work as an army nurse in South Africa. She saw this as a way of eventually returning to West Africa. Her application was at first turned down, on the grounds that the war 'would all be over in no time'.

The Royal Geographical Society building in London. This was the headquarters for British exploration, but when Mary Kingsley had returned from Africa the society still did not allow women members.

THE BOER WARS

Descendants of Dutch settlers in South Africa were called Boers (Dutch for farmers). At the end of the 19th century, southern Africa was part of the British **Empire**. Two wars (known as the first and second Boer Wars) broke out between the British government forces and the Boers, who rebelled against British rule. The Boers were eventually defeated in 1902 and their territories were united with the British provinces to form one Union of South Africa.

Trench warfare in the Boer War. Soldiers on both sides were fighting in terrible conditions, and there were many casualties from disease as well as gunfire.

The beginning of 1900 was a particularly quiet and lonely time for Kingsley. She had no book to work on and saw little of her friends. Her lecture schedule had also quietened down considerably. Then the War Office contacted her again to say her application to work as a nurse had been accepted. She was expected to leave for South Africa early in March.

Throughout February, Kingsley made preparations for her departure. She picked up another set of fish-collecting equipment from Dr Günther and also signed up as a **war correspondent** for two newspapers, the *Morning Post* and the *Evening News*. By early March everything was ready.

On the evening of Friday 4 March she had supper with Charley. Early the next morning, Kingsley and her great friend Alice Green travelled by train from London to the port of Southampton. As the train gathered speed, Kingsley could feel the ties that had held her down for the past five years gradually loosening. She was leaving England once again, this time for a war thousands of miles away. Deep down she must have wondered if she would ever return.

In Mary Kingsley's words:

'Goodbye and fare you well, for I am homeward bound.'

(Said at the end of one of her last lectures, given in February 1900)

A nurse once more

The dock at Southampton was crowded with soldiers, cases of ammunition, guns and food supplies. Kingsley boarded a troopship called the *Moor* as one of the few civilians on board. As Southampton slipped out of sight, Kingsley waved to the solitary figure of Alice Green still standing on the pier.

A source of strength

All the years Kingsley had tended others meant she was very well prepared to work as a nurse, even though she had never received any formal training. On board the *Moor* were 650 soldiers and other military personnel, as well as two brass bands. Every available space was crammed with supplies and there was very little water and ventilation inside the ship. These conditions, and the poor diet of tinned pork and fish, combined to make many of the soldiers very ill within days of leaving England. The further south they sailed, the hotter the weather became and this only added to their problems.

RUDYARD KIPLING

Soon after arriving in South Africa, Kingsley got to know Rudyard Kipling (1865–1936), who was living nearby. He was a very famous **journalist**, poet and short-story writer and while in South Africa he covered the Boer War. He and Kingsley struck up a close friendship and he described her as 'the bravest woman of all my knowledge'.

Rudyard Kipling was one of the most famous and popular British writers at this time. He had fallen seriously ill from pneumonia and had gone to South Africa to rest.

The *Moor* soon resembled a hospital ship and Kingsley spent most of her time looking after the sick soldiers. Several had developed **pneumonia** and one died and had to be buried at sea. Kingsley was rushing around with little help and few medical supplies. As the ship crossed the Bay of Biscay, a rough sea meant many soldiers now fell ill from seasickness.

On 28 March, after a journey of eighteen days, the *Moor* finally reached Cape Town, South Africa. Kingsley immediately reported to General Wilson, chief medical officer of Cape **Colony**, to find out where she would be sent. Rather than working with British troops, Kingsley was assigned as a nurse to the large number of sick and wounded Boer soldiers. She was sent to a temporary hospital set up in the Palace Barracks in nearby Simonstown.

In Mary Kingsley's words:

'The rest of society [the soldiers on the Moor*] and myself have coughed at each other and arrived at a reasonable understanding of each other, but Oh! for a saloon full of palm oil ruffians.'*

(A letter from Kingsley to Alice Green describing her journey to South Africa. While sailing round the coast of West Africa, Kingsley had often travelled with traders of palm oil.)

The British Hotel in Simonstown at about the time Kingsley arrived there in 1900. The town was small and elegant with tree-lined streets surrounding Simonstown Bay.

Death in South Africa

When Kingsley arrived at the 'Palace', as the Simonstown hospital was known, the entire staff consisted of only one doctor and three nurses, of which Kingsley was one. By the end of April, two more doctors and three more nurses had joined, but these numbers were pitifully inadequate for the 200 patients in the hospital.

The last few months

Most of the patients were survivors from a terrible battle at a site called Paardeberg. Many had contracted **typhoid fever** – some were unconscious, others so feverish they were **delirious** and threw themselves from their beds. The hospital wards were filthy and the patients lay on iron beds. For two months, Kingsley and the other nurses worked all day and night to help relieve the sufferings of the soldiers. Kingsley did much more than nurse her patients. She talked to them and listened to them as they spoke about their fears, so they began to regard her as a friend rather than an English nurse.

The stench in the hospital wards was terrible and the walls and floors were covered with bugs and lice. Towards the end of May, Kingsley herself caught **enteric fever**. Her heart had already been weakened from her illness two years before in England.

The Palace Barracks in Simonstown. It was converted into a hospital during the Boer War and Mary worked there as a nurse treating wounded Boer soldiers.

The fever got worse and Kingsley had to be operated on. However, it was too late and on 3 June 1900 Kingsley died peacefully in her sleep from heart failure. She was just 37 years old.

Mary Kingsley's coffin was taken from the hospital and placed on a gun-carriage. A huge crowd of people turned out for the funeral procession from the hospital to Simonstown Bay, including members of the Boer community. Kingsley never did return to England, for she had given strict instructions that her body was to be buried at sea off the coast of her beloved Africa rather than in the family grave in London. Her coffin was placed on board a small ship and taken out to sea. As the coffin slipped beneath the waves, the people on board watched in silence and saluted this great woman.

In the words of a friend:

'She was so unassuming, so unaffected, such a womanly woman in every sense of the word ... '

'The truest, kindest, staunchest friend that ever breathed – such was Mary Kingsley.'

(Both written by the London **journalist** Edmund Morel)

Mary Kingsley's funeral procession. The poor quality of the photograph shows that it was not taken by a professional photographer, but perhaps by one of the many people who attended the funeral.

The legacy of Mary Kingsley

When the news of Kingsley's death reached Britain, the whole country went into mourning. Since the publication of her first book, *Travels in West Africa*, she had become one of the most famous people in the country. However, now, 100 years later, the name of Mary Kingsley is almost forgotten.

The title page of Mary Kingsley's best-selling first book, published in 1897.

TRAVELS
IN WEST AFRICA

Congo Français, Corisco and Cameroons

BY
MARY H. KINGSLEY

WITH ILLUSTRATIONS

London
MACMILLAN AND CO., Limited
NEW YORK: THE MACMILLAN COMPANY
1897

All rights reserved

How important was Mary Kingsley's work? She was more of a traveller than an explorer, although she did cross parts of Gabon that had never been visited by Europeans before. During her time in West Africa she lived a life of incredible adventure, excitement and also danger. But it cannot be said that she really 'discovered' this part of Africa for Europeans in the way that others such as Mungo Park and David Livingstone had done before her.

In the area of African politics Kingsley's contribution is also slight, for she failed in many of the tasks that she had set herself on her return to England in 1895. However, her influence on the development of West Africa at the end of the 19th century and first half of the 20th has been far-reaching. She confronted the politicians of the day about the accepted European view of superiority over Africa and its people. Her determination eventually helped to break down prejudice. She fought for the rights of African people and this contributed to the independence movement of the African nations in the second half of the 20th century.

As the author of *Travels in West Africa* and *West African Studies*, Mary Kingsley wrote two of the most interesting and beautiful works of travel literature in the English language. She was one of the greatest of all the great women of **Victorian** England. She never set out to champion the cause of the women's movement, but through her honesty, bravery and determination she showed just what it was possible for women to achieve, at a time when they were expected to do nothing except raise families behind closed doors.

A photograph of Mary Kingsley taken in 1897, at the time Travels in West Africa *was published.*

Map of Mary Kingsley's journeys

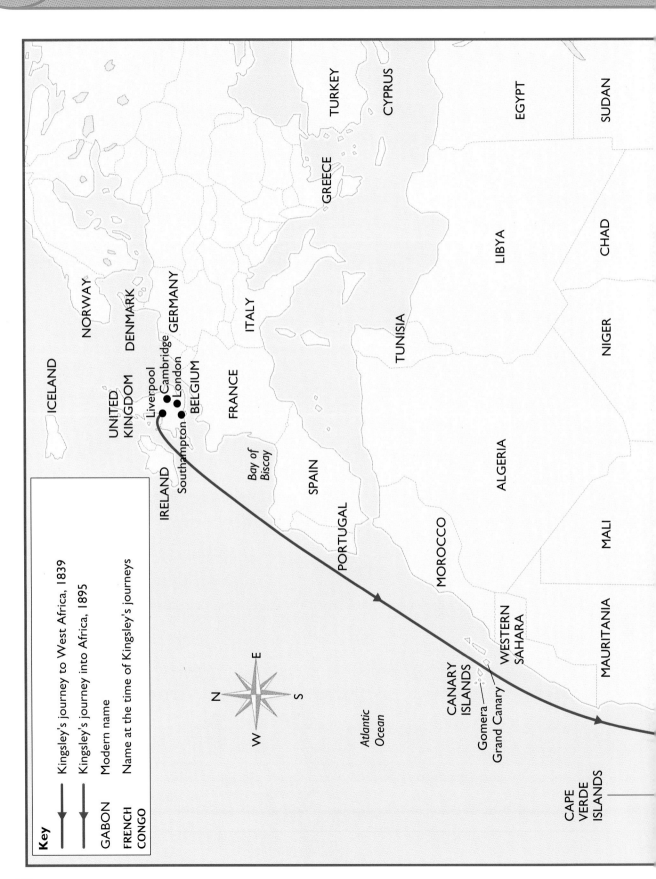

Key

→	Kingsley's journey to West Africa, 1839
→	Kingsley's journey into Africa, 1895
GABON	Modern name
FRENCH CONGO	Name at the time of Kingsley's journeys

ICELAND

NORWAY

DENMARK

UNITED KINGDOM

IRELAND

Liverpool
Cambridge
London
Southampton

GERMANY

BELGIUM

FRANCE

Bay of Biscay

ITALY

GREECE

TURKEY

CYPRUS

EGYPT

SUDAN

LIBYA

CHAD

NIGER

SPAIN

PORTUGAL

MOROCCO

TUNISIA

ALGERIA

MALI

MAURITANIA

WESTERN SAHARA

CANARY ISLANDS

Gomera
Grand Canary

Atlantic Ocean

CAPE VERDE ISLANDS

N E S W

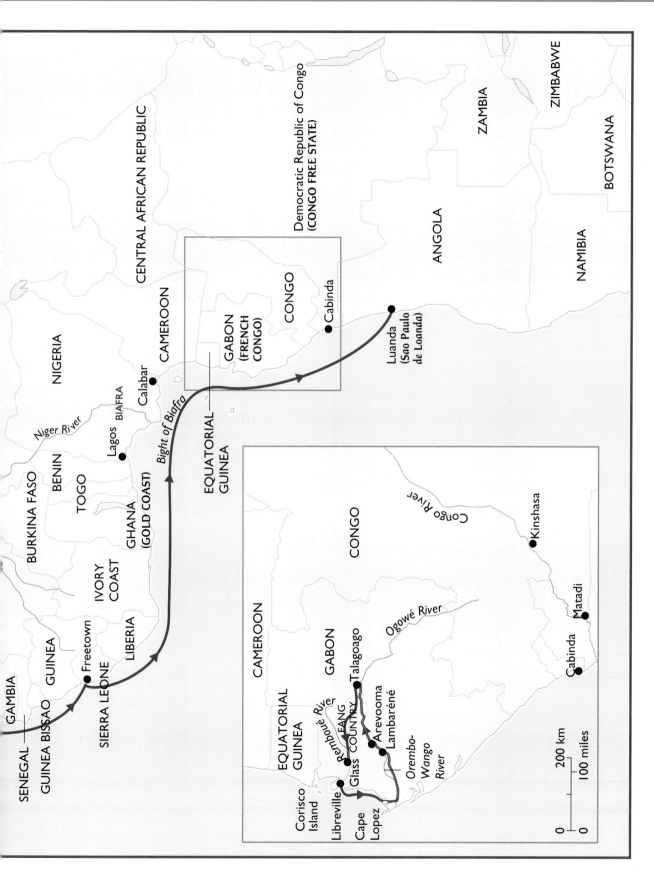

SENEGAL
GAMBIA
GUINEA BISSAO
GUINEA
SIERRA LEONE
Freetown
LIBERIA
IVORY COAST
BURKINA FASO
BENIN
TOGO
GHANA (GOLD COAST)
Niger River
NIGERIA
Lagos
BIAFRA
Calabar
Bight of Biafra
CAMEROON
EQUATORIAL GUINEA
CENTRAL AFRICAN REPUBLIC
GABON (FRENCH CONGO)
CONGO
Cabinda
Democratic Republic of Congo (CONGO FREE STATE)
Luanda (Sao Paulo de Loanda)
ANGOLA
ZAMBIA
ZIMBABWE
BOTSWANA
NAMIBIA

CAMEROON
EQUATORIAL GUINEA
Corisco Island
Libreville
GABON
Rembouë River
FANG COUNTRY
Glass
Cape Lopez
Talagoago
Arevooma
Lambaréné
Orembo-Wango River
Ogowé River
CONGO
Congo River
Kinshasa
Matadi
Cabinda

0   200 km
0   100 miles

43

Timeline

1862	Marriage of George Kingsley and Mary Bailey.
	Birth of their daughter Mary.
1869	Diamond rush begins in South Africa.
	Opening of Suez Canal in Egypt.
1871	David Livingstone, missing for four years, discovered alive by Henry Stanley in East Africa.
1877	Queen Victoria proclaimed Empress of India.
	Transvaal, South Africa, annexed (taken over) by Britain.
1880–81	First Boer War.
1884	Germany takes South West Africa, Cameroons and Togo; Britain takes British Somaliland.
1885	Germany takes Tanganyika; Italy, Eritrea; Belgium, Belgian Congo; Britain, Bechuanaland; Spain, Rio de Oro and Spanish Guinea.
1886	Lagos (on Nigerian coast) becomes a British **colony**.
1888	Mary Kingsley makes her first trip abroad, to Paris.
1888–89	Rhodesia becomes a British colony.
1888	The French take Ivory Coast; the Italians take Somaliland.
1892	Mary Kingsley's parents die.
	She travels to the Canary Islands.
1893	She leaves on her first trip to West Africa.
1894	She begins her second expedition to West Africa.
	The French annex Dahomey.
1895	Britain takes Uganda.
1896	The French annex Madagascar.
1897	Mary Kingsley's *Travels in West Africa* published.
1899	Her *West African Studies* published.
1899–1902	Second Boer War.
1900	Mary Kingsley travels to South Africa.
	Death of Mary Kingsley.
1910	Britain forms Union of South Africa.

Places to visit
British Museum, London
Commonwealth Institute, London
Natural History Museum, London

Websites
www.thebritishmuseum.ac.uk
www.thehistorychannel.co.uk
www.thetravelbookshop.co.uk
www.enchantedlearning.com

Further reading
On the Trail of the Victorians in Britain, Peter Chrisp (Franklin Watts, 1999)
Uncommon Traveler: Mary Kingsley in Africa, Don Brown (Houghton Mifflin, 2000))
Victorian Britain (History of Britain series), Andrew Langley (Heinemann Libary, 1994)
Victorian Family Life (History of Britain Topic Books), Jane Shuter (Heinemann Library, 1997)
The Victorians (Heritage series), Robert Hall (Hodder Wayland, 2000)

Sources
Mary Kingsley, Dea Birkett (Macmillan, 1992)
Travels in West Africa, Mary Kingsley (Everyman Classic, 1987)
West African Studies, Mary Kingsley (London, 1899)
A Victorian Lady in Africa, Valerie Myer (Ashford Press, 1989)
A Voyager Out, Katherine Frank (Hamish Hamilton, 1987)

Glossary

archaeologist someone who studies the past by examining remains left by humans, such as buildings and pottery

cannibal person who eats the flesh of other humans

chore routine job, especially a domestic household task

clergyman Christian preacher or religious worker

colony area or territory taken over by people from outside that area

commission officially request to perform a duty or job

delirious mentally confused, often because of illness

empire very large group of territories and people across a wide area under the rule of a single person or government

enteric fever disease of the intestines which causes fever

Far East group of countries made up of China, Japan and other east Asian countries

foothills low hills lying at the foot of a mountain

illegitimate born to parents who are not married. In the Victorian period this would not have been acceptable to many people.

indigenous people who are local or 'native' to a particular country or area. They are born in that country usually and have many generations of relatives who were also born there.

journalist person who writes news stories for newspapers or magazines

learned society organization dedicated to the study of academic subjects

menagerie collection of animals

middle class section of society consisting of professional and business people and their families

missionary person who is a member of a religious group sent to do religious and social work

novelist writer of novels, or works of fiction

paddle steamer boat powered by both paddles and steam

philosophy way of thinking about truth and reality in the world

physician someone who practises medicine

pneumonia inflammation of one or both lungs

practice office where a profession such as medicine or law is carried out

prospector person who searches for gold, precious stones, petroleum, and other materials that are mined

rapids steep, rocky part of a river with fast-moving water

rheumatic fever disease characterized by inflammation and pain in the joints

social reformer someone who tries to change conditions in society for the better, usually to relieve the suffering of the sick and poor

stroke rupture of a blood vessel in the brain resulting in a loss of consciousness and often followed by paralysis

tornado violent storm with whirling winds that can cause great damage

typhoid fever serious infectious disease characterized by high fever, spots and stomach pain

Victorian the period during the reign of Queen Victoria (1837–1901)

war correspondent someone who sends reports from a war zone, usually for publication in newspapers or magazines

War Office government department making decisions in times of war

working class section of society consisting of people who work for others in return for wages, for example in factories

zoology the study of animals

Index

African artefacts 20, 21

Batty, James 13
Boer Wars 34, 35
Bruce, James 31

Caillié, René 31
Calabar 19, 22. 23. 30
Cambridge 9
Canary Islands 12–13
Chamberlain, Joseph 33
colonialism 4, 33
Congo Free State (Democratic Republic of Congo) 18
Congo River 24
Corisco 28

Dennett, Richard 18

Fang people 26, 27, 28
Fernando Po 22
Freetown 17
French Congo (Gabon) 4, 18, 19, 24–8, 40

Glass 19, 25, 28
Gomera 13
Green, Alice 35, 36
Günther, Dr Albert 14, 21, 25, 35

Kingsley, Charles (uncle) 6
Kingsley, Charley (brother) 4, 7, 8, 14, 15, 20, 21, 34, 35
Kingsley, Dr George (father) 4, 6, 8, 9, 11, 12
Kingsley, Henry (uncle) 6
Kingsley, Mary
   achievements 40–1
   and African people 5, 33, 40
   army nursing 34, 35, 36, 37, 38
   birth and early life 4, 6–8
   Canary Islands trip 12–13

criticizes British rule in Africa 5, 32, 33, 40
   education 8
   family 4, 6–11
   first trip abroad 10
   illnesses and death 33, 38–9
   lectures 32, 34, 35
   personal qualities 5, 39, 41
   photographs and portraits of 4, 5, 8, 11, 22, 41
   public acclaim 4, 30–1
   in South Africa 36–9
   travel writing 4, 5, 20, 32, 33, 40, 41
   war correspondent 35
   West African travels 15–20, 22–30, 40, 42–3
Kingsley, Mary Bailey (mother) 4, 6, 7, 8, 10, 11
Kipling, Rudyard 36

Lagos 24
Libreville 19
Liverpool 15
Livingstone, David 31, 40
Luanda 17, 18

MacDonald, Lady 21, 22, 23
MacDonald, Sir Claude 19, 22, 23
missionaries 23, 26, 31
Mount Cameroon 29

Natural History Museum 14, 31
Niger River 24, 28

Ogowé River 24, 25, 26

Paris 10
Park, Mungo 31, 40

Remboué River 26, 27, 28
Royal Geographical Society 34

'scramble for Africa' 4, 33
Sierra Leone 17
Simonstown 37, 38
Slessor, Mary 23, 30
South Africa 34, 35, 36–9
Stanley, Henry 31

Throne of Thunder 29

women's education 8, 9

Titles in the *Groundbreakers* series include:

Hardback　　　0 431 10489 1

Hardback　　　0 431 10490 5

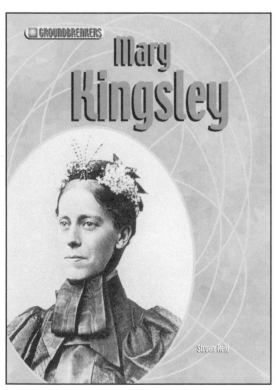

Hardback　　　0 431 10491 3

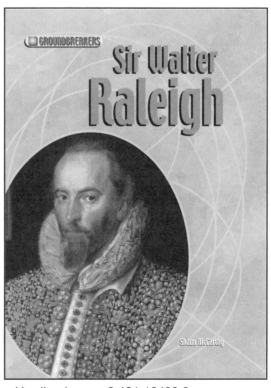

Hardback　　　0 431 10488 3

Find out about the other titles in this series on our website www.heinemann.co.uk/library